AF413524

WHAT IS THE GREATEST COMMON FACTOR

Math Workbooks Grade 6

Children's Math Books

Speedy Publishing LLC

40 E. Main St. #1156

Newark, DE 19711

www.speedypublishing.com

Copyright 2017

All Rights reserved. No part of this book may be reproduced or used in any way or form or by any means whether electronic or mechanical, this means that you cannot record or photocopy any material ideas or tips that are provided in this book.

WHAT IS A FACTOR?

Factors are numbers you can multiply together to get another number.

FINDING THE GREATEST
COMMON FACTOR!

Find the Greatest Common Factor for each number pair.

1) 6 , 4   **2**

2) 3 , 2 _____

3) 24 , 4 _____

4) 12 , 6 _____

5) 12 , 4 _____

6) 12 , 4 _____

7) 4 , 2 _____

8) 6 , 3 _____

9) 3 , 12 _____

10) 24 , 4 _____

Find the Greatest Common Factor for each number pair.

1)   6 , 8 ______

2)   24 , 8 ______

3)   4 , 2 ______

4)   24 , 3 ______

5)   6 , 8 ______

6)   6 , 12 ______

7)   4 , 3 ______

8)   12 , 2 ______

9)   2 , 6 ______

10)   12 , 3 ______

Find the Greatest Common Factor for each number pair.

1)   4 , 2   _______

2)   6 , 12   _______

3)   12 , 24   _______

4)   8 , 3   _______

5)   3 , 2   _______

6)   2 , 24   _______

7)   2 , 8   _______

8)   4 , 3   _______

9)   12 , 3   _______

10)   3 , 24   _______

Find the Greatest Common Factor for each number pair.

1)   6 , 2   ______

2)   12 , 4   ______

3)   2 , 4   ______

4)   8 , 24   ______

5)   12 , 24   ______

6)   4 , 3   ______

7)   12 , 8   ______

8)   2 , 8   ______

9)   6 , 2   ______

10)   3 , 24   ______

Find the Greatest Common Factor for each number pair.

1) 24 , 6 ______

2) 2 , 6 ______

3) 8 , 6 ______

4) 2 , 3 ______

5) 12 , 24 ______

6) 6 , 2 ______

7) 8 , 3 ______

8) 8 , 2 ______

9) 3 , 4 ______

10) 24 , 8 ______

Find the Greatest Common Factor for each number pair.

1)   2 , 24   _______

2)   3 , 8   _______

3)   8 , 24   _______

4)   3 , 6   _______

5)   8 , 24   _______

6)   12 , 2   _______

7)   6 , 24   _______

8)   24 , 2   _______

9)   12 , 3   _______

10)   24 , 4   _______

Find the Greatest Common Factor for each number pair.

1)   6 , 3   _____

2)   2 , 8   _____

3)   24 , 2   _____

4)   8 , 4   _____

5)   4 , 8   _____

6)   6 , 24   _____

7)   6 , 24   _____

8)   12 , 6   _____

9)   2 , 24   _____

10)   8 , 3   _____

Find the Greatest Common Factor for each number pair.

1) 8 , 24 _____

2) 2 , 24 _____

3) 6 , 12 _____

4) 24 , 8 _____

5) 8 , 2 _____

6) 12 , 4 _____

7) 3 , 12 _____

8) 6 , 8 _____

9) 24 , 12 _____

10) 8 , 6 _____

EXERCISE 8

Find the Greatest Common Factor for each number pair.

1)   2 , 3   _____

2)   24 , 6   _____

3)   3 , 12   _____

4)   2 , 4   _____

5)   8 , 3   _____

6)   4 , 2   _____

7)   8 , 4   _____

8)   8 , 12   _____

9)   24 , 8   _____

10)   8 , 6   _____

Find the Greatest Common Factor for each number pair.

1) 2 , 24 ______

2) 8 , 3 ______

3) 8 , 6 ______

4) 12 , 3 ______

5) 4 , 24 ______

6) 8 , 3 ______

7) 8 , 4 ______

8) 12 , 24 ______

9) 6 , 12 ______

10) 4 , 6 ______

Find the Greatest Common Factor for each number pair.

EXERCISE 11

1)   5 , 12 ______

2)   3 , 15 ______

3)   5 , 8 ______

4)   20 , 4 ______

5)   40 , 24 ______

6)   2 , 10 ______

7)   2 , 12 ______

8)   3 , 20 ______

9)   8 , 24 ______

10)   24 , 20 ______

Find the Greatest Common Factor for each number pair.

1)   10 , 5   _______

2)   10 , 5   _______

3)   6 , 30   _______

4)   15 , 4   _______

5)   8 , 4   _______

6)   2 , 40   _______

7)   2 , 3   _______

8)   8 , 10   _______

9)   8 , 3   _______

10)   4 , 6   _______

Find the Greatest Common Factor for each number pair.

1) 10 , 12 _______

2)   8 , 30 _______

3) 24 , 2 _______

4)   3 , 20 _______

5) 15 , 40 _______

6) 30 , 6 _______

7)   3 , 2 _______

8)   2 , 20 _______

9)   2 , 20 _______

10) 15 , 30 _______

Find the Greatest Common Factor for each number pair.

1)   30 , 20 _____

2)   20 , 30 _____

3)   10 , 6 _____

4)   2 , 24 _____

5)   3 , 24 _____

6)   30 , 20 _____

7)   5 , 15 _____

8)   8 , 40 _____

9)   30 , 8 _____

10)   10 , 40 _____

Find the Greatest Common Factor for each number pair.

1) 15 , 30 ______

2) 15 , 3 ______

3) 30 , 6 ______

4) 6 , 24 ______

5) 12 , 2 ______

6) 6 , 5 ______

7) 24 , 3 ______

8) 8 , 5 ______

9) 12 , 40 ______

10) 30 , 15 ______

Find the Greatest Common Factor for each number pair.

1) 2 , 15 _____

2) 24 , 3 _____

3) 8 , 4 _____

4) 30 , 12 _____

5) 4 , 8 _____

6) 15 , 6 _____

7) 10 , 4 _____

8) 8 , 4 _____

9) 15 , 20 _____

10) 60 , 5 _____

Find the Greatest Common Factor for each number pair.

1) 4 , 24 _______

2) 30 , 10 _______

3) 30 , 20 _______

4) 60 , 4 _______

5) 20 , 3 _______

6) 5 , 12 _______

7) 20 , 4 _______

8) 12 , 24 _______

9) 8 , 10 _______

10) 5 , 8 _______

Find the Greatest Common Factor for each number pair.

1) 24 , 30 _______

2)   8 , 6 _______

3)   3 , 6 _______

4)   3 , 8 _______

5)   3 , 12 _______

6)   2 , 15 _______

7) 30 , 12 _______

8) 30 , 10 _______

9) 10 , 30 _______

10)   8 , 24 _______

Find the Greatest Common Factor for each number pair.

1)   12 , 30   _______

2)   30 , 5   _______

3)   20 , 24   _______

4)   10 , 15   _______

5)   60 , 8   _______

6)   8 , 6   _______

7)   4 , 20   _______

8)   30 , 5   _______

9)   12 , 3   _______

10)   3 , 12   _______

Find the Greatest Common Factor for each number pair.

1) 10 , 15 _______

2) 8 , 10 _______

3) 2 , 60 _______

4) 15 , 8 _______

5) 40 , 20 _______

6) 10 , 2 _______

7) 3 , 2 _______

8) 4 , 10 _______

9) 8 , 20 _______

10) 20 , 3 _______

Find the Greatest Common Factor for each number pair.

1)   2 , 20   _______

2)   5 , 15   _______

3)   2 , 24   _______

4)   8 , 40   _______

5)   2 , 30   _______

6)   15 , 24   _______

7)   4 , 3   _______

8)   5 , 40   _______

9)   2 , 30   _______

10)   5 , 6   _______

Find the Greatest Common Factor for each number pair.

1)　　6 , 30　　______

2)　　4 , 3　　______

3)　　5 , 15　　______

4)　　8 , 20　　______

5)　　6 , 20　　______

6)　　4 , 20　　______

7)　　4 , 20　　______

8)　　3 , 6　　______

9)　　5 , 40　　______

10)　　30 , 15　　______

Find the Greatest Common Factor for each number pair.

1)   5 , 24   ______

2)   10 , 12   ______

3)   24 , 6   ______

4)   3 , 12   ______

5)   15 , 6   ______

6)   30 , 10   ______

7)   60 , 12   ______

8)   40 , 3   ______

9)   20 , 30   ______

10)   30 , 20   ______

Find the Greatest Common Factor for each number pair.

1) 10 , 8 _______

2) 20 , 2 _______

3) 2 , 20 _______

4) 20 , 5 _______

5) 3 , 30 _______

6) 40 , 10 _______

7) 20 , 30 _______

8) 30 , 15 _______

9) 30 , 5 _______

10) 8 , 3 _______

1)   4 , 60   _______

2)   4 , 12   _______

3)   12 , 4   _______

4)   2 , 5   _______

5)   20 , 10   _______

6)   10 , 15   _______

7)   2 , 20   _______

8)   5 , 60   _______

9)   40 , 4   _______

10)   3 , 40   _______

Find the Greatest Common Factor for each number pair.

1) 10 , 8 ______

2) 60 , 20 ______

3) 5 , 6 ______

4) 8 , 24 ______

5) 40 , 2 ______

6) 4 , 20 ______

7) 6 , 30 ______

8) 3 , 8 ______

9) 5 , 24 ______

10) 10 , 2 ______

Find the Greatest Common Factor for each number pair.

1) 120 , 30 _______

2) 24 , 15 _______

3) 4 , 3 _______

4) 15 , 12 _______

5) 6 , 24 _______

6) 6 , 120 _______

7) 40 , 12 _______

8) 15 , 60 _______

9) 24 , 2 _______

10) 120 , 4 _______

Find the Greatest Common Factor for each number pair.

1)   8 , 4   _______

2)   10 , 15   _______

3)   8 , 20   _______

4)   6 , 2   _______

5)   2 , 120   _______

6)   15 , 40   _______

7)   6 , 60   _______

8)   8 , 24   _______

9)   2 , 24   _______

10)   5 , 24   _______

Find the Greatest Common Factor for each number pair.

1) 5 , 30 _______

2) 20 , 8 _______

3) 5 , 24 _______

4) 15 , 12 _______

5) 20 , 60 _______

6) 40 , 12 _______

7) 10 , 5 _______

8) 30 , 8 _______

9) 24 , 4 _______

10) 6 , 30 _______

EXERCISE

29

Find the Greatest Common Factor for each number pair.

1)　60 , 30　_____

2)　20 , 6　_____

3)　6 , 12　_____

4)　5 , 3　_____

5)　3 , 8　_____

6)　120 , 15　_____

7)　3 , 15　_____

8)　30 , 10　_____

9)　2 , 120　_____

10)　10 , 4　_____

Find the Greatest Common Factor for each number pair.

1) 10 , 12 ______

2) 2 , 3 ______

3) 30 , 15 ______

4) 6 , 3 ______

5) 6 , 15 ______

6) 30 , 2 ______

7) 20 , 10 ______

8) 4 , 10 ______

9) 40 , 10 ______

10) 2 , 12 ______

Find the Greatest Common Factor for each number pair.

1) 6 , 12 ______

2) 15 , 30 ______

3) 60 , 15 ______

4) 12 , 20 ______

5) 60 , 20 ______

6) 15 , 3 ______

7) 60 , 40 ______

8) 8 , 40 ______

9) 30 , 3 ______

10) 2 , 3 ______

Find the Greatest Common Factor for each number pair.

1)   5 , 3   ______

2)   60 , 20   ______

3)   4 , 5   ______

4)   12 , 6   ______

5)   2 , 24   ______

6)   6 , 40   ______

7)   24 , 40   ______

8)   12 , 5   ______

9)   60 , 5   ______

10)   10 , 20   ______

Find the Greatest Common Factor for each number pair.

1) 30 , 24 ______

2) 40 , 30 ______

3) 30 , 10 ______

4) 120 , 15 ______

5) 60 , 3 ______

6) 120 , 20 ______

7) 20 , 10 ______

8) 60 , 15 ______

9) 2 , 12 ______

10) 12 , 3 ______

Find the Greatest Common Factor for each number pair.

1) 3 , 10 _______

2) 3 , 12 _______

3) 20 , 10 _______

4) 20 , 40 _______

5) 5 , 30 _______

6) 20 ,120 _______

7) 6 , 8 _______

8) 120 , 40 _______

9) 3 , 6 _______

10) 8 , 30 _______

LET'S LEARN MORE ABOUT FACTORS!

List all the factors of each number.

1) 39 1, 3, 13, 39

2) 51 ______________________________

3) 68 ______________________________

4) 63 ______________________________

5) 77 ______________________________

6) 45 ______________________________

7) 78 ______________________________

8) 28 ______________________________

9) 65 ______________________________

10) 33 ______________________________

List all the factors of each number.

1) 44 _______________________

2) 57 _______________________

3) 42 _______________________

4) 69 _______________________

5) 36 _______________________

6) 51 _______________________

7) 15 _______________________

8) 24 _______________________

9) 28 _______________________

10) 78 _______________________

List all the factors of each number.

1) 56 __________________________

2) 16 __________________________

3) 75 __________________________

4) 39 __________________________

5) 70 __________________________

6) 72 __________________________

7) 49 __________________________

8) 76 __________________________

9) 21 __________________________

10) 26 __________________________

List all the factors of each number.

1) 50 _______________________________

2) 38 _______________________________

3) 45 _______________________________

4) 25 _______________________________

5) 10 _______________________________

6) 64 _______________________________

7) 51 _______________________________

8) 22 _______________________________

9) 26 _______________________________

10) 48 _______________________________

List all the factors of each number.

1) 25 ______________________________

2) 12 ______________________________

3) 49 ______________________________

4) 39 ______________________________

5) 34 ______________________________

6) 27 ______________________________

7) 76 ______________________________

8) 22 ______________________________

9) 42 ______________________________

10) 74 ______________________________

List all the factors of each number.

EXERCISE 41

1) 27 _______________________________

2) 45 _______________________________

3) 76 _______________________________

4) 12 _______________________________

5) 55 _______________________________

6) 20 _______________________________

7) 70 _______________________________

8) 32 _______________________________

9) 57 _______________________________

10) 36 _______________________________

List all the factors of each number.

1) 40 _______________________________

2) 48 _______________________________

3) 49 _______________________________

4) 66 _______________________________

5) 44 _______________________________

6) 68 _______________________________

7) 39 _______________________________

8) 50 _______________________________

9) 46 _______________________________

10) 70 _______________________________

List all the factors of each number.

1) 16 ______________________________

2) 10 ______________________________

3) 57 ______________________________

4) 12 ______________________________

5) 14 ______________________________

6) 15 ______________________________

7) 34 ______________________________

8) 62 ______________________________

9) 39 ______________________________

10) 64 ______________________________

List all the factors of each number.

1) 46 _______________________________

2) 64 _______________________________

3) 68 _______________________________

4) 51 _______________________________

5) 45 _______________________________

6) 57 _______________________________

7) 76 _______________________________

8) 25 _______________________________

9) 55 _______________________________

10) 75 _______________________________

ANSWERS!

1)   6 , 4   2
2)   3 , 2   1
3)   24 , 4   4
4)   12 , 6   6
5)   12 , 4   4
6)   12 , 4   4
7)   4 , 2   2
8)   6 , 3   3
9)   3 , 12   3
10)   24 , 4   4

1)   6 , 8   2
2)   24 , 8   8
3)   4 , 2   2
4)   24 , 3   3
5)   6 , 8   2
6)   6 , 12   6
7)   4 , 3   1
8)   12 , 2   2
9)   2 , 6   2
10)   12 , 3   3

1)   4 , 2   2
2)   6 , 12   6
3)   12 , 24   12
4)   8 , 3   1
5)   3 , 2   1
6)   2 , 24   2
7)   2 , 8   2
8)   4 , 3   1
9)   12 , 3   3
10)   3 , 24   3

1)   6 , 2   2
2)   12 , 4   4
3)   2 , 4   2
4)   8 , 24   8
5)   12 , 24   12
6)   4 , 3   1
7)   12 , 8   4
8)   2 , 8   2
9)   6 , 2   2
10)   3 , 24   3

<table>
<tr><td colspan="2">

EXERCISE 5

</td><td colspan="2">

EXERCISE 6

</td></tr>
</table>

1) 24 , 6 6	1) 2 , 24 2
2) 2 , 6 2	2) 3 , 8 1
3) 8 , 6 2	3) 8 , 24 8
4) 2 , 3 1	4) 3 , 6 3
5) 12 , 24 12	5) 8 , 24 8
6) 6 , 2 2	6) 12 , 2 2
7) 8 , 3 1	7) 6 , 24 6
8) 8 , 2 2	8) 24 , 2 2
9) 3 , 4 1	9) 12 , 3 3
10) 24 , 8 8	10) 24 , 4 4

<table>
<tr><td colspan="2">

EXERCISE 7

</td><td colspan="2">

EXERCISE 8

</td></tr>
</table>

1) 6 , 3 3	1) 8 , 24 8
2) 2 , 8 2	2) 2 , 24 2
3) 24 , 2 2	3) 6 , 12 6
4) 8 , 4 4	4) 24 , 8 8
5) 4 , 8 4	5) 8 , 2 2
6) 6 , 24 6	6) 12 , 4 4
7) 6 , 24 6	7) 3 , 12 3
8) 12 , 6 6	8) 6 , 8 2
9) 2 , 24 2	9) 24 , 12 12
10) 8 , 3 1	10) 8 , 6 2

<table>
<tr><td>

1)   2 , 3   __1__

2)   24 , 6   __6__

3)   3 , 12   __3__

4)   2 , 4   __2__

5)   8 , 3   __1__

6)   4 , 2   __2__

7)   8 , 4   __4__

8)   8 , 12   __4__

9)   24 , 8   __8__

10)   8 , 6   __2__

</td><td>

1)   2 , 24   __2__

2)   8 , 3   __1__

3)   8 , 6   __2__

4)   12 , 3   __3__

5)   4 , 24   __4__

6)   8 , 3   __1__

7)   8 , 4   __4__

8)   12 , 24   __12__

9)   6 , 12   __6__

10)   4 , 6   __2__

</td></tr>
<tr><td>

1)   5 , 12   __1__

2)   3 , 15   __3__

3)   5 , 8   __1__

4)   20 , 4   __4__

5)   40 , 24   __8__

6)   2 , 10   __2__

7)   2 , 12   __2__

8)   3 , 20   __1__

9)   8 , 24   __8__

10)   24 , 20   __4__

</td><td>

1)   10 , 5   __5__

2)   10 , 5   __5__

3)   6 , 30   __6__

4)   15 , 4   __1__

5)   8 , 4   __4__

6)   2 , 40   __2__

7)   2 , 3   __1__

8)   8 , 10   __2__

9)   8 , 3   __1__

10)   4 , 6   __2__

</td></tr>
</table>

<table>
<tr><td colspan="2">

EXERCISE 13

</td><td colspan="2">

EXERCISE 14

</td></tr>
<tr><td>

1) 10 , 12   <u>2</u>

</td><td></td><td>

1) 30 , 20   <u>10</u>

</td><td></td></tr>
</table>

EXERCISE 13

1) 10 , 12   <u>2</u>

2) 8 , 30   <u>2</u>

3) 24 , 2   <u>2</u>

4) 3 , 20   <u>1</u>

5) 15 , 40   <u>5</u>

6) 30 , 6   <u>6</u>

7) 3 , 2   <u>1</u>

8) 2 , 20   <u>2</u>

9) 2 , 20   <u>2</u>

10) 15 , 30   <u>15</u>

EXERCISE 14

1) 30 , 20   <u>10</u>

2) 20 , 30   <u>10</u>

3) 10 , 6   <u>2</u>

4) 2 , 24   <u>2</u>

5) 3 , 24   <u>3</u>

6) 30 , 20   <u>10</u>

7) 5 , 15   <u>5</u>

8) 8 , 40   <u>8</u>

9) 30 , 8   <u>2</u>

10) 10 , 40   <u>10</u>

EXERCISE 15

1) 15 , 30   <u>15</u>

2) 15 , 3   <u>3</u>

3) 30 , 6   <u>6</u>

4) 6 , 24   <u>6</u>

5) 12 , 2   <u>2</u>

6) 6 , 5   <u>1</u>

7) 24 , 3   <u>3</u>

8) 8 , 5   <u>1</u>

9) 12 , 40   <u>4</u>

10) 30 , 15   <u>15</u>

EXERCISE 16

1) 2 , 15   <u>1</u>

2) 24 , 3   <u>3</u>

3) 8 , 4   <u>4</u>

4) 30 , 12   <u>6</u>

5) 4 , 8   <u>4</u>

6) 15 , 6   <u>3</u>

7) 10 , 4   <u>2</u>

8) 8 , 4   <u>4</u>

9) 15 , 20   <u>5</u>

10) 60 , 5   <u>5</u>

<table>
<tr><td colspan="2">

EXERCISE 17

</td><td colspan="2">

EXERCISE 18

</td></tr>
</table>

	EXERCISE 17		EXERCISE 18
1)	4 , 24 4	1)	24 , 30 6
2)	30 , 10 10	2)	8 , 6 2
3)	30 , 20 10	3)	3 , 6 3
4)	60 , 4 4	4)	3 , 8 1
5)	20 , 3 1	5)	3 , 12 3
6)	5 , 12 1	6)	2 , 15 1
7)	20 , 4 4	7)	30 , 12 6
8)	12 , 24 12	8)	30 , 10 10
9)	8 , 10 2	9)	10 , 30 10
10)	5 , 8 1	10)	8 , 24 8

	EXERCISE 19		EXERCISE 20
1)	12 , 30 6	1)	10 , 15 5
2)	30 , 5 5	2)	8 , 10 2
3)	20 , 24 4	3)	2 , 60 2
4)	10 , 15 5	4)	15 , 8 1
5)	60 , 8 4	5)	40 , 20 20
6)	8 , 6 2	6)	10 , 2 2
7)	4 , 20 4	7)	3 , 2 1
8)	30 , 5 5	8)	4 , 10 2
9)	12 , 3 3	9)	8 , 20 4
10)	3 , 12 3	10)	20 , 3 1

EXERCISE 21		EXERCISE 22	
1)	2 , 20 2	1)	6 , 30 6
2)	5 , 15 5	2)	4 , 3 1
3)	2 , 24 2	3)	5 , 15 5
4)	8 , 40 8	4)	8 , 20 4
5)	2 , 30 2	5)	6 , 20 2
6)	15 , 24 3	6)	4 , 20 4
7)	4 , 3 1	7)	4 , 20 4
8)	5 , 40 5	8)	3 , 6 3
9)	2 , 30 2	9)	5 , 40 5
10)	5 , 6 1	10)	30 , 15 15

EXERCISE 23		EXERCISE 24	
1)	5 , 24 1	1)	10 , 8 2
2)	10 , 12 2	2)	20 , 2 2
3)	24 , 6 6	3)	2 , 20 2
4)	3 , 12 3	4)	20 , 5 5
5)	15 , 6 3	5)	3 , 30 3
6)	30 , 10 10	6)	40 , 10 10
7)	60 , 12 12	7)	20 , 30 10
8)	40 , 3 1	8)	30 , 15 15
9)	20 , 30 10	9)	30 , 5 5
10)	30 , 20 10	10)	8 , 3 1

EXERCISE 25

1)   4 , 60   __4__

2)   4 , 12   __4__

3)   12 , 4   __4__

4)   2 , 5   __1__

5)   20 , 10   __10__

6)   10 , 15   __5__

7)   2 , 20   __2__

8)   5 , 60   __5__

9)   40 , 4   __4__

10)   3 , 40   __1__

EXERCISE 26

1)   10 , 8   __2__

2)   60 , 20   __20__

3)   5 , 6   __1__

4)   8 , 24   __8__

5)   40 , 2   __2__

6)   4 , 20   __4__

7)   6 , 30   __6__

8)   3 , 8   __1__

9)   5 , 24   __1__

10)   10 , 2   __2__

EXERCISE 27

1)   120 , 30   __30__

2)   24 , 15   __3__

3)   4 , 3   __1__

4)   15 , 12   __3__

5)   6 , 24   __6__

6)   6 , 120   __6__

7)   40 , 12   __4__

8)   15 , 60   __15__

9)   24 , 2   __2__

10)   120 , 4   __4__

EXERCISE 28

1)   8 , 4   __4__

2)   10 , 15   __5__

3)   8 , 20   __4__

4)   6 , 2   __2__

5)   2 , 120   __2__

6)   15 , 40   __5__

7)   6 , 60   __6__

8)   8 , 24   __8__

9)   2 , 24   __2__

10)   5 , 24   __1__

EXERCISE 29

1) 5 , 30 __5__

2) 20 , 8 __4__

3) 5 , 24 __1__

4) 15 , 12 __3__

5) 20 , 60 __20__

6) 40 , 12 __4__

7) 10 , 5 __5__

8) 30 , 8 __2__

9) 24 , 4 __4__

10) 6 , 30 __6__

EXERCISE 30

1) 60 , 30 __30__

2) 20 , 6 __2__

3) 6 , 12 __6__

4) 5 , 3 __1__

5) 3 , 8 __1__

6) 120 , 15 __15__

7) 3 , 15 __3__

8) 30 , 10 __10__

9) 2 , 120 __2__

10) 10 , 4 __2__

EXERCISE 31

1) 10 , 12 __2__

2) 2 , 3 __1__

3) 30 , 15 __15__

4) 6 , 3 __3__

5) 6 , 15 __3__

6) 30 , 2 __2__

7) 20 , 10 __10__

8) 4 , 10 __2__

9) 40 , 10 __10__

10) 2 , 12 __2__

EXERCISE 32

1) 6 , 12 __6__

2) 15 , 30 __15__

3) 60 , 15 __15__

4) 12 , 20 __4__

5) 60 , 20 __20__

6) 15 , 3 __3__

7) 60 , 40 __20__

8) 8 , 40 __8__

9) 30 , 3 __3__

10) 2 , 3 __1__

EXERCISE 33		EXERCISE 34	
1) 5 , 3 __1__		1) 30 , 24 __6__	
2) 60 , 20 __20__		2) 40 , 30 __10__	
3) 4 , 5 __1__		3) 30 , 10 __10__	
4) 12 , 6 __6__		4) 120 , 15 __15__	
5) 2 , 24 __2__		5) 60 , 3 __3__	
6) 6 , 40 __2__		6) 120 , 20 __20__	
7) 24 , 40 __8__		7) 20 , 10 __10__	
8) 12 , 5 __1__		8) 60 , 15 __15__	
9) 60 , 5 __5__		9) 2 , 12 __2__	
10) 10 , 20 __10__		10) 12 , 3 __3__	

EXERCISE 35		EXERCISE 36	
1) 3 , 10 __1__		1) 39 1 , 3 , 13, 39	
2) 3 , 12 __3__		2) 51 1 , 3 , 17, 51	
3) 20 , 10 __10__		3) 68 1 , 2 , 4 , 17, 34, 68	
4) 20 , 40 __20__		4) 63 1 , 3 , 7 , 9 , 21, 63	
5) 5 , 30 __5__		5) 77 1 , 7 , 11, 77	
6) 20 , 120 __20__		6) 45 1 , 3 , 5 , 9 , 15, 45	
7) 6 , 8 __2__		7) 78 1 , 2 , 3 , 6 , 13, 26, 39, 78	
8) 120 , 40 __40__		8) 28 1 , 2 , 4 , 7 , 14, 28	
9) 3 , 6 __3__		9) 65 1 , 5 , 13, 65	
10) 8 , 30 __2__		10) 33 1 , 3 , 11, 33	

EXERCISE 37

1) 44 1 , 2 , 4 , 11, 22, 44

2) 57 1 , 3 , 19, 57

3) 42 1 , 2 , 3 , 6 , 7 , 14, 21, 42

4) 69 1 , 3 , 23, 69

5) 36 1 , 2 , 3 , 4 , 6 , 9 , 12, 18, 36

6) 51 1 , 3 , 17, 51

7) 15 1 , 3 , 5 , 15

8) 24 1 , 2 , 3 , 4 , 6 , 8 , 12, 24

9) 28 1 , 2 , 4 , 7 , 14, 28

10) 78 1 , 2 , 3 , 6 , 13, 26, 39, 78

EXERCISE 38

1) 56 1 , 2 , 4 , 7 , 8 , 14, 28, 56

2) 16 1 , 2 , 4 , 8 , 16

3) 75 1 , 3 , 5 , 15, 25, 75

4) 39 1 , 3 , 13, 39

5) 70 1 , 2 , 5 , 7 , 10, 14, 35, 70

6) 72 1 , 2 , 3 , 4 , 6 , 8 , 9 , 12, 18, 24, 36, 72

7) 49 1 , 7 , 49

8) 76 1 , 2 , 4 , 19, 38, 76

9) 21 1 , 3 , 7 , 21

10) 26 1 , 2 , 13, 26

EXERCISE 39

1) 50 1 , 2 , 5 , 10, 25, 50

2) 38 1 , 2 , 19, 38

3) 45 1 , 3 , 5 , 9 , 15, 45

4) 25 1 , 5 , 25

5) 10 1 , 2 , 5 , 10

6) 64 1 , 2 , 4 , 8 , 16, 32, 64

7) 51 1 , 3 , 17, 51

8) 22 1 , 2 , 11, 22

9) 26 1 , 2 , 13, 26

10) 48 1 , 2 , 3 , 4 , 6 , 8 , 12, 16, 24, 48

EXERCISE 40

1) 25 1 , 5 , 25

2) 12 1 , 2 , 3 , 4 , 6 , 12

3) 49 1 , 7 , 49

4) 39 1 , 3 , 13, 39

5) 34 1 , 2 , 17, 34

6) 27 1 , 3 , 9 , 27

7) 76 1 , 2 , 4 , 19, 38, 76

8) 22 1 , 2 , 11, 22

9) 42 1 , 2 , 3 , 6 , 7 , 14, 21, 42

10) 74 1 , 2 , 37, 74

<table>
<tr><td colspan="2">

EXERCISE 41

</td><td colspan="2">

EXERCISE 42

</td></tr>
<tr><td>1)</td><td>27</td><td>1 , 3 , 9 , 27</td></tr>
</table>

EXERCISE 41

1)	27	1 , 3 , 9 , 27
2)	45	1 , 3 , 5 , 9 , 15, 45
3)	76	1 , 2 , 4 , 19, 38, 76
4)	12	1 , 2 , 3 , 4 , 6 , 12
5)	55	1 , 5 , 11, 55
6)	20	1 , 2 , 4 , 5 , 10, 20
7)	70	1 , 2 , 5 , 7 , 10, 14, 35, 70
8)	32	1 , 2 , 4 , 8 , 16, 32
9)	57	1 , 3 , 19, 57
10)	36	1 , 2 , 3 , 4 , 6 , 9 , 12, 18, 36

EXERCISE 42

1)	40	1 , 2 , 4 , 5 , 8 , 10, 20, 40
2)	48	1 , 2 , 3 , 4 , 6 , 8 , 12, 16, 24, 48
3)	49	1 , 7 , 49
4)	66	1 , 2 , 3 , 6 , 11, 22, 33, 66
5)	44	1 , 2 , 4 , 11, 22, 44
6)	68	1 , 2 , 4 , 17, 34, 68
7)	39	1 , 3 , 13, 39
8)	50	1 , 2 , 5 , 10, 25, 50
9)	46	1 , 2 , 23, 46
10)	70	1 , 2 , 5 , 7 , 10, 14, 35, 70

EXERCISE 43

1)	16	1 , 2 , 4 , 8 , 16
2)	10	1 , 2 , 5 , 10
3)	57	1 , 3 , 19, 57
4)	12	1 , 2 , 3 , 4 , 6 , 12
5)	14	1 , 2 , 7 , 14
6)	15	1 , 3 , 5 , 15
7)	34	1 , 2 , 17, 34
8)	62	1 , 2 , 31, 62
9)	39	1 , 3 , 13, 39
10)	64	1 , 2 , 4 , 8 , 16, 32, 64

EXERCISE 44

1)	46	1 , 2 , 23, 46
2)	64	1 , 2 , 4 , 8 , 16, 32, 64
3)	68	1 , 2 , 4 , 17, 34, 68
4)	51	1 , 3 , 17, 51
5)	45	1 , 3 , 5 , 9 , 15, 45
6)	57	1 , 3 , 19, 57
7)	76	1 , 2 , 4 , 19, 38, 76
8)	25	1 , 5 , 25
9)	55	1 , 5 , 11, 55
10)	75	1 , 3 , 5 , 15, 25, 75

Visit
BABY PROFESSOR
EDUCATION KIDS
www.BabyProfessorBooks.com
to download Free Baby Professor eBooks
and view our catalog of new and exciting
Children's Books

www.ingramcontent.com/pod-product-compliance
Lightning Source LLC
Chambersburg PA
CBHW081355150726
48196CB00005BA/500